I Spy

Written by Joe Elliot
Illustrated by Neil Sutherland, Blue-Zoo and Tony Trimmer

"Can we play a game?" asked W.
"I like to play I Spy," replied I.
W was delighted.

"I will start!" cried **W**. "I spy something
beginning with I!"
"Is it me?" asked **I**, with a smile.

"Why, yes!" cried **W**. "Now you have a go!"
"I spy something beginning with W," said **I**.
"Is it me?" asked **W**.

"No," replied I. "It is water!"

"Water?" replied W. "Where?"

"It is there!" said I, pointing.

"I think we need to try something different," said I, kindly. "Hold my hand!"

w - i - l - d , wild!
I tried to be wild.
"I do not feel wild!" she said, with a sigh.

Suddenly, they were in the wild!
"I like the wild!" said I.

"I spy something beginning with B!"
said **D**.

"Butterflies!" cried I.

B was flying by with five butterflies!

"I spy something beginning with C!" said W.
"And I spy something beginning with T!"
cried D.

C was riding by on a crocodile.
"Crikey! This is fun!" she said.

T was tickling a tiger.
"I spy something beginning with L!" said L.

"It is a lion!" said L. "And he thinks
we are his dinner!"
"Hide!" cried W.

They hid from the lion.
"How do we escape?" asked **D**.
Then **K** and **E** came to help.

k - i - t - e, kite! They got a kite.
"I spy something beginning with E!" said **I**.
"The End!" said **W**.